SPIRITU

A SEARCH FOR BALANCE AND ENLIGHTENMENT

JUSTIN ALBERT

Copyright © 2014 by Justin Albert

Why You Should Read This Book

This book will reveal the ancient techniques of spirituality on your search to better your interior life. Spirituality has long been the stronghold of humanity; it has provided purpose in the midst of unrest, violence, war, and terror. With this book, you can learn several non-religious techniques that reveal inner peace, that work to nurture you and allow you to find your true life purpose. Through ancient meditative practices, ideas of pilgrimage, the concept of mindfulness, Yoga poses, and an understanding of the Buddhist concept of Enlightenment, you can thrive with your inner self and refute the rushing, chaotic nature of your surrounding world. You can take charge of your life once more. Understand how spiritual healing can complete your physical, internal healing and promote your immune system. Furthermore, look to this book for a backdrop of both religious and non-religious practices of spirituality throughout the incredible tradition of humanity. Understand the ways in which the world has found comfort and strength for thousands of years, and work to achieve your own sense of your personal journey today.

Why You Should Read This Book

Chapter 1. 9
  The Importance and History of Spirituality 9
  The Importance of Spirituality 9
    Overcoming Hardships 10
    Making Healthier Choices 11
    Living Longer and More Fruitfully......................................12
    Forgiving and Letting Go 12
  The History of Spirituality 13
    Paleolithic Spirituality 13
    Paleolithic Spiritual Contacting..15
  Small Scale Spirituality Versus Large-Scale Spirituality:
  Today's Religious Sectors..15
    The Spiritual Key of the Past..17

Chapter 2. 19
  THE ROAD TO MINDFULNESS 19
  What is Mindfulness? 19
    History of Mindfulness: Buddhism and Anapanasati.........19
  Benefits of Mindfulness..21
  How to Achieve Mindfulness 24

Chapter 3. MEDITATION..27
  Brief History of Meditation...27
  Proper Meditation Techniques 28
    Creating Mind Stillness 29

Chapter 4. YOGA: TECHNIQUES AND HISTORICAL
CONTEXT..33
  History of Yoga 33
    The Vedic Period..34
    Pre-Classical Yoga 34

    The Classical Period 35
    Post-Classical Yoga..35
  Yoga Poses and Benefits 36
    Dandasana or Staff Pose..36
    Marjaryasana or Cat pose..37
    Uttanasana or Standing Forward Bend...............................37
    Salamba Sirsasana or Head Stand with Support................38

Chapter 5. FINDING INNER PEACE 40
  Self-Actualization 40

Chapter 6. 44

ACHIEVING ENLIGHTENMENT........................ 44
    Buddhism and Nirvana 45
  Achieve Enlightenment Today 45
  The Zen Mind 51
    Observe the Mind and Observe the Breath........................51
    The Koan Practice 52

Chapter 7. SPIRITUAL HEALING 54
  Engage in Spiritual Healing 54
    Therapeutic Touch 55
    Reiki 55
  Spirituality: A Conclusion 56

About The Author 57

Other Books By Justin Albert............................ 59
  Free preview of 59

Why You Should Read This Book 60

Chapter 1. Motivation: The Only Road to Greatness...... 62
  What is Motivation? 63

Definition of Motivation 63
Three Components of Motivation 64
A Life Without Motivation: What Happens? 66
Feelings of Failure and Inadequacy 66

Chapter 2. Theories of Motivation 69
Drive Theory 69
Homeostasis: Balance and Equilibrium 69
Instinct Theory 70
What Is An Instinct? 70
Maslow's Hierarchy of Needs 70
Stage 1: Physiological Needs 71
One Last Thing 74

Chapter 1.

The Importance and History of Spirituality

Humanity has long linked itself to a greater purpose, a higher power. And this "higher power" takes so many different forms across separate centuries, across different peoples, and across altering opinions. This "higher power" could take the form of a supreme creator, a transcendental state of being, or simply some sort of magical force. The overall strength behind this higher power, however, is the existence of spirituality. Spirituality is the linking element between all greater peoples, that which allows humanity comfort in the overall struggle that is general, everyday life. Even people with a lack of religious doctrine feel spirituality through yoga, meditation, private prayer, and long walks through nature. Skeptics of spirituality can't stifle the sense that there's something "greater" than humanity. The skeptical brain and the religious brain are continually looking for patterns in the world, in the people met along the road of life. Through these patterns, the brain attempts to create meaning. And because of something called "cognitive dissonance," the brain can eliminate those things in life that do not align with this spiritual, patterned world. The brain can create a meaning all its own.

The Importance of Spirituality

Life holds a series of traumas. Being born, for example, is one of the most traumatic dilemmas in a person's life, and things get rocky from there. Childhood is a constant battle through confusion, through feelings of being "too little," and adulthood reveals no sense of assuredness. Humanity is born, it grows, and it dies without any real, concrete understanding of: why.

Holding a strong feeling of spirituality, however, can help a person push beyond the great struggles of life. This feeling can bring meaning to seemingly incomprehensible scenarios: death, divorce, war, violence, and imprisonment. It helps a person to care for his inner being by allowing himself to believe in something greater, overarching. It allows a person to give himself a purpose in life. He can believe that everything he's done has been for a reason, that creating a life for himself has not been for naught. He leaves this feeling in his family line after he moves on to the "next world," allowing his spouse and his children to feel this warmth and comfort of spirituality as well. This spirituality can come in the form of a specific religion. Alternately, it can simply be a mindful belief in inner peace, in the concept of the present moment's strength.

Overcoming Hardships

With spirituality in tow, a person can refute the challenges of life traumas. As mentioned previously, life churns with war, violence, and other hardships—things seemingly without purpose, without a greater sense of spirituality. However, with a spiritual outlook, a person can peg meaning to these great life dilemmas and move forward with his life, allowing himself to build from this terrible adjustment.

An example finds a woman reeling in the trauma of a violent divorce. Finally, after years of beating, she felt the power to leave. It's true that her spirituality allowed her to find the strength to look for something better for herself. Her spirituality led her from the grasp of sure evils. However, her spirituality further allows her to believe, after the trauma, that the trauma had a greater purpose in her life. Instead of feeling immense anger at her husband and the harm he had caused her, she is able to reach beyond anger, find forgiveness, and find reason for the terrible trauma. She is able to evaluate her life and change her life for the better. However, if she had lacked that spirituality, she might have lingered on in the traumatic environment or continually felt complete anger at the trauma in the years after. With anger and hatred, she would not have the ability to grow.

With spirituality comes the feeling of an "interconnectedness" of reality. This interconnectedness can allow a person to feel that nothing happens without purpose, as outlined above. This feeling can actually buffer the pain of daily life, allowing a person to feel compassion toward himself in the light of failure. A person can remind himself that failure is a shared human experience, one that draws all humanity together. A person does not have to feel lonely.

MAKING HEALTHIER CHOICES

With spirituality in tow, a person makes more ready healthy decisions regarding his body and mind. Many spiritual traditions, for example, hold high rules about bringing strict kindness to the body. A person is meant to avoid unhealthy behaviors. For example, one of the seven deadly sins in Christianity is "gluttony," which is overeating, while other

am, make strict rules against the
 alcohol. Furthermore, several religious
 k toward a decrease in violent activity and
 vity. With the feeling of a higher power, people
 ely to be involved in smoking, and are further
more   ly to wear their seatbelts while driving. Why is this, exactly? Essentially, the lack of hope associated with a lack of spirituality or belief in a higher power leads a person to believe in the "now or never" mentality. Therefore, speeding down the highway without a seatbelt, eating a piece of cake or two every day, and binge drinking seem like no trouble in the span of his day-to-day life.

Living Longer and More Fruitfully

Scientists agree: there is an essential relationship between prolonged life and spiritual practices. Giancario Lucchetti conducted a study to analyze mortality in relation to spirituality and found that people with an ingrained view of a higher power lived about 18% longer than those without spirituality. Lucchetti asserts that spirituality is so much like eating fruits and vegetables and maintaining your medications. It is an essential part of every day life.

Forgiving and Letting Go

Several religious doctrines and spiritual traditions promote the practice of forgiveness, and for good reason. As a person releases blame and negative feelings, he receives lower blood pressure, a better immunity, greater cardiovascular health, and a fuller, more vibrant life. As mentioned above, when a person releases anger, he can begin to focus on why the event that caused the anger occurred in relation to his life. He can begin to rebuild and see more purpose in himself.

The History of Spirituality

Spirituality history stems from a several thousand-year history. Because humans are the only beings on the planet with language, they are the only ones who can transmit ideas of right versus wrong, who can bring about a sense of the "spiritual" world. They utilize symbolic language to talk about a higher realm, a higher order. These languages yield ideas of demons, fairies, gods, angels, heaven, and hell.

Different languages and thus different communities, however, have built several different ideas about their spiritual worlds. Through the years, people have fought wars and killed millions in order to keep their spiritual world ideas intact. One community's spirituality can hold completely different ideas than another community's ideas. For example, some communities in the world have nudity traditions; others, on the other hand, hold high crimes against nudity based on spiritual or religious doctrines.

Paleolithic Spirituality

The history of spirituality stems from long ago. Look back to fifteen thousand years ago in southern Europe. People made the painstaking journey through a great cave in order to carve small clay figurines of bison. These people probably understood that these bison figurines would never be seen by their peers, by anyone. They had no concept for 20th century archaeology, of course. Why, then, did they carve the bison? The carving was not for pure enjoyment; it was not for art's sake. Furthermore, there are several worldwide cave paintings of hunters and animals. A theory aligning with these paintings is that they were drawn to sort of "cast a magic spell" over the animals for easy capture. A cave in Europe in particular reveals some sort of figure that resembles a wizard. However, there is no way to know who this mystical figure really was.

Anthropologists have so little ready knowledge about the Paleolithic realm and therefore can bring about only a little knowledge about the actual spiritual environment of that time. In order to bring better ideas of the Paleolithic spiritual era, the anthropologists have begun studying the current spiritual beliefs of certain isolated communities. Anthropologists reason that these communities maintain the same thought processes and behaviors as human Paleolithic ancestors because of their lack of growth into the modern world.

Anthropologists have found that there is generally no real, inlaid boundary between these communities' spiritual worlds and human worlds. This is demonstrated with the idea of animism. Animism is the belief many of these communities hold that they must coexist and communicate with the spirits that live alongside of them. They feel that they must ally with the spirits, bargain with the spirits, and generally respect them in order to fuel themselves through life.

These communities often find natural forces and beings like wind, rain, trees, thunder, the moon, and the sun to be members of a great, natural family of spirits meant to be bargained with and lived alongside. Oftentimes, these spirits are both good and bad and hold similar moral dilemmas as natural humans. Think of, for example, the Ancient Greek gods and their perpetual sexual affairs with other gods and humans. The Greeks regarded these spiritual beings as reckless creatures that they had to obey in order to survive.

Alternately, some families or clans have the idea that their family has an undeniable link to some sort of animal. For example, if a family feels itself "linked" to the groups of elephants, they may forbid killing them. Feeling a link to greater formations of society is an absolute form of spirituality.

Paleolithic Spiritual Contacting

From anthropologist studies of current isolated communities, they've deduced how Paleolithic communities probably contacted their personal spiritual worlds. The communities may contact spirits through rituals or feel their communion through dreams. Certain religious ceremonies involve dancing, mind-altering drugs, or chanting. They hope to feel the spirits alongside them. Oftentimes, these communities seek a representative from their midst. These people are "gifted" in their communication with the various spirits. For example, Siberia boasts such specialists known as shamans. The shamans go into a sort of trance and rush into the spiritual realm in order to discuss something with the spirits. Sometimes, these discussions turn to anger. Sometimes, they turn to pleading. Sometimes, alternately, they result in the shaman marrying a spirit. What the shamans learn from these spirits can alter the state of an entire community. The knowledge can spur communities to go into war or charge toward greater peace.

Small-Scale Spirituality Versus Large-

Scale Spirituality: Today's Religious Sectors

Prior to about 12,000 B.C., spirituality was a local phenomenon. For example, spirits were like local friends and very particular to small communities. However, as communities began to grow into larger societies, the spirits became more powerful. Gradually, people like priests took the place of "shamans" and were said to have spiritual powers. Rulers were associated with powerful deities and ultimately said they were, themselves, gods. Pharaohs of ancient Egypt, for example, thought themselves to be reincarnations of the Sun God, Rah.

Quite obviously, the seeds of countless spiritual sects grew through several thousands of years, resulting in countless belief systems. Later, from these religions, grew the major universalist religions of today. These include: Christianity, Buddhism, Hinduism, Daoism, and Islam. Judaism is still very prevalent in today's spirituality; however, it is not considered a universalist religion because it only considers the descendants of the early religion to be Jewish. It's important to note, however, that Judaism shares a god with both Christianity and Islam.

As mentioned previously, each religion has various practices and belief systems that allow their practicing members to exist in the human world with an assurance of a spiritual world, as well. None of the religions are completely homogenous; for example, the Christian tradition holds within it Catholics, Greek Catholics, Lutherans, Baptists, and countless other sects that reach toward spirituality in new and different ways all the time.

Generally, many of these religions bring two integral dimensions. One involves public worship: all the practicing religious people coming together for communal prayer and congregation. This brings a sense of community on the search for spirituality. The other dimension of religion yields something far more personal—and covered in this book at length. This is the interior search for a person's religious "spirit"—a person's God, a person's feeling of transcendence. Both the interior search and the communion-rich search for spirituality bring about an engrained sense of life meaning, of deeper purpose in the greater world.

Most notably, this idea of animism, outlined previously, has not completely disintegrated in these very modern religions—bringing the idea that everyone worships precisely in the ways he needs to. For example, small Christian communities throughout the world may honor a certain local saint. This saint is much like their version of an ancient spirit. Furthermore, small Muslim communities occasionally wear a small box around their neck. The small box contains a piece of paper with words from their religious text, the Qur'an. Their reason? The box wards off evil. The very Qur'an in their box, however, condones the practice of "warding off demons" in this manner.

The Spiritual Key of the Past

At human history's very core is the concept of religious and spiritual practices. These practices allow humanity to have a better understanding of the surrounding world; they allow humanity to mold into a better, more structured community of people working side-by-side toward the same goal. Through their spirituality, people everywhere have been able to find meaning in order to build their futures. Successful communities full of spiritual people have enjoyed greater peace and cooperation.

However, the greatest benefit of spirituality lies on the individual level. Within yourself.

Chapter 2.
The Road to Mindfulness

What is Mindfulness?

The concept of mindfulness is the overall acceptance of one's full attention to one's thoughts, emotions, and intricate sensations during the very present moment. Furthermore, as one notices one's thoughts and feelings, one does not judge them. One fully accepts these feelings as a part of one's self, without pegging the thoughts with concepts of "right" or "wrong." The topic holds its roots in Buddhist practices.

History of Mindfulness: Buddhism and Anapanasati

One of the derivatives of today's mindfulness is the concept of Anapanasati in Buddhism. Anapanasati means "mindfulness of breathing," and it is a style of Buddhist meditation. Currently, it is practiced in Tibetan, Zen, Theravada, and Tiantai Buddhist schools. Anapanasati means that a person feels all the sensations caused as the person breaths in and breaths out.

According to Buddhist tradition, Anapanasati allows a person to cultivate the seven factors of awakening through the analysis of breathing. These seven factors are: sati, which means mindfulness; dhamma vicaya, which means analysis; viriya, which means persistence; piti, which means rapture; passaddhi, which means serenity; Samadhi, which means concentration; and ultimately upekkha, which means equanimity. These seven factors are arrived at in this precise order to achieve complete release from suffering. A person utilizing this process who achieved this release from suffering was said to have realized Nirvana—the ultimate goal of the Buddhist path.

The traditional, ancient practice of anapanasati involved a person removing himself from the society and sitting beneath a tree in the forest. He was simply meant to breathe and notice what occurred. As he breathed, he was to notice, for example, if his breath was long. If it was long, he was meant to accept it. If the breath was short, he was meant to accept this. As he continued to breathe, he was meant to practice and work his mind. He was meant to train his mind to be more in tune with his body, his feelings of rapture, his feelings of pleasure, and his interior mental processes. He was further meant to practice steadying his mind, satisfying his mind, and completely releasing his mind from his grasp.

Modern takes on this anapanasati asks a person to sit alone, in a cool, dark location. This person is meant to count his exhalations in initial cycles of ten. Afterwards, he is meant to count his inhalations in initial cycles of ten. Next, he is meant to focus on his breathing without counting a single breath. Finally, he is meant to focus his mind solely on the area in which the breath enters and exits his body: simply his nostrils.

According to Buddhist practices, mindfulness is simply a presence of mind, a complete attention to the present moment, without a glimmer of confusion. It holds no notion of memory. However, it also allows the person to hold awareness of something to be recollected after the meditation state. For example, a person is meant to recollect something he must do at some point in the future. This is in relation to meditating with a desire to loosen a person's grasp on drug addictions; it is further related to a person's trials to reach a certain goal in his life through mindfulness and attentiveness to his body. Through mindfulness, he must recollect—at a later time—his goals and his greater life affirming qualities. He must remember his awareness while also being aware.

Furthermore, Buddhism states that present-day mindfulness works toward the three marks of existence. These three marks are: impermanence, the unsatisfactory nature of everything that exists on this current planet, and the feeling of non-self.

BENEFITS OF MINDFULNESS

Practicing mindfulness shows elements of psychological, social, and physiological benefits.

1. *MINDFULNESS AND IMMUNITY.*

   Studies show that after eight weeks of practicing daily mindfulness, the body elevates its immune system's functionality. Therefore, it is more in tune with warding off diseases. This could be, of course, because people tend to begin thinking more about what they ingest, what they place on their bodies, and what they "get themselves into." However, allowing the mind to calm down further contributes to an elevated interiority and reduced interior inflammation.

2. *MINDFULNESS AND THE BRAIN.*

Just a few days of mindfulness can increase the positive emotions flowing in the brain's neural pathways. Negative emotions and stress levels decrease, as well. Stress levels, when too high, are actually detrimental to your overall health. The stress hormone, cortisol, is the fight or flight hormone, the very element that allowing humanity to survive so much of the natural world. However, when cortisol runs rampant in the system, it can begin to destroy the hippocampus brain cells. The hippocampus is the part of the brain that makes brand new brain cells and switches short-term memories to long-term memories.

3. *MINDFULNESS AND CHANGING BRAIN MATTER.*

   Furthermore, daily mindfulness can increase brain functionality. The brain's gray matter density increases, thus allowing greater memory, learning, empathy, and emotion regulation to occur. With these increased capabilities, a person can live a truly enriched lifestyle.

4. *MINDFULNESS AND FOCUS.*

   With mindfulness, the brain can filter out what it doesn't "need" to think about in the moment. Therefore, as a person works on a very specific project, the brain can tune out certain distractions and become completely attentive.

5. *MINDFULNESS AND COMPASSION.*

   As previously mentioned, compassion is one of the very necessary elements allowing a group of people to formulate a thriving community. Therefore, with greater compassion and altruism swimming in a mindful brain, a person is at-the-ready to assist needy people. Furthermore, a person can actively understand and empathize with the suffering of others. Research further shows that self-compassion, or a desire to keep one's self well, is boosted as well. Isn't that the type of world a person should work toward—a world of renewed compassion?

6. *MINDFULNESS AND RELATIONSHIPS.*

When a person utilizes mindfulness alongside a partner, the couple reports maintaining a more fulfilled relationship. Each partner feels more relaxed, more optimistic about the future. Furthermore, and perhaps most importantly, the couple feels closer to each other than ever.

7. *MINDFULNESS AND PARENTING.*

Parents and parents-to-be who practice mindfulness show signs of reduced anxiety, depression, and stress. Furthermore, current parents find themselves satisfied with their parenting habits and their relationships. The children have flourishing social lives outside of the household, as well.

8. *MINDFULNESS AND SCHOOLS.*

Bringing mindfulness into the classroom actually reduces student aggression and student unhappiness. Furthermore, it boosts their ability to be attentive to the lessons while reducing their behavioral problems. Teachers who actively associate with mindfulness further have lower blood pressure and greater compassion. They are less likely to show signs of depression.

9. *MINDFULNESS AND PRISONS.*

    Mindfulness activation in prisons reduces strange moods and hostility among prisoners. The prisoners become completely aware of their emotions and begin to work toward better rehabilitation.

10. *MINDFULNESS AND VETERANS.*

    A veteran who practices daily mindfulness has a lower risk of Post Traumatic Stress Disorder in the years after his war days.

11. *MINDFULNESS AND OBESITY.*

    Mindfulness and eating go hand in hand. As a person practices mindful eating, he begins to understand his eating habits and the ways in which he can begin to lose weight. Furthermore, he can begin to savor his food—further enjoying his life.

HOW TO ACHIEVE MINDFULNESS

You don't have to utilize the strict Buddhist maneuvers in order to create mindfulness in your daily life. You must simply begin to notice your life in all its beauty, in all its simplicity. Follow the key components of mindfulness practice listed below.

1. Think about your thoughts and your emotions. Notice them as an outsider, and realize this: they are fleeing from you at all times. All your negative thoughts, all your disgraceful thoughts—everything: they're flying from you at a quick rate, and they do not define you. Therefore, you can eliminate negative thoughts and work toward more

positive thinking. Don't allow your negative thoughts to define you. They are in the moment, and then they are lost.

2. As outlined above, you must pay very close attention to your breathing habits. When your emotions seem at their critical height, try to notice only your breathing. Bring your thoughts, your feelings, to your nostrils and feel the air pass through them. Count your breaths.

3. Work hard to notice every single moment of your life. You won't be getting the moment back. It is here—and then it is gone. Your brain is so finely tuned to recognizing sounds, sights, and smells, and your consciousness is so used to dismissing them. Allow yourself to sense each and every one the bad ones and the good.

4. Feel all physical sensations. Feel the shower water hitting you in the morning and the way the water dribbles down your leg. Feel your body resting in the body, the way it feels to jostle to the right and to the left. Understand how each movement brings a different physical feeling to your body.

Chapter 3. Meditation

Meditation, in its current state, is a loose and imprecise word. People throw it around, utilizing it to describe their daydream state or their afternoon contemplation about what's for dinner. However, meditation is a very specific utensil for creating a more restful, more spiritual life.

Meditation allows a person to rest the mind and bring a sense of eternal consciousness that is different from everyday, normal consciousness. While in a meditative state, a person is able to bring an understanding of each and every level of himself. He can see all he has done and all he is capable of. Furthermore, meditation allows him to experience the very center of his interior consciousness; he is able to come to an understanding of how he fits into the greater universe.

While meditating, a person is completely relaxed with an inward focus. He is awake, attentive; however, his mind is not alert to the exterior world. Meditation brings an idea of an inner state: one that allows the whirring mind to finally stand still. Essentially, a person can transcend his thoughts and his distraction in order to find a deeper sense of spiritual reality.

Brief History of Meditation

As mentioned previously, spirituality holds its roots in the prehistoric era. Meditation stems back to these early years, to the age of chanting and rhythmic repetitions. Today, of course, these are called "mantras."

The earliest record of meditation is found in 1500 BCE. It is rooted in the Hindu tradition; however, it further found its way to Taoist China and Buddhist India. As seen in the previous chapter, meditation is a true element of mindfulness in the early Buddhist teachings. Sitting in a cool, dark location, one is meant to reach beyond one's "whirring" mind to find a sense of non-self.

Today, meditation is used as a tool for spiritual growth and stress reduction. After so many thousands of years, however, scientists are still unsure about the exact mechanisms for meditation's wonderful benefits. It has, quite clearly, fueled countless generations of spiritual beings in religion after religion. It is a form of prayer, a reach to an "outer" understanding. And today, it can be both secular and religious. Regardless, it brings assuredness in a chaotic world.

Proper Meditation Techniques

Childhood life teaches a person to look to the external world in order to education himself. Teachers and parents point out the strangeness of the world, and a person is meant to compare himself to this externality. However, no one teaches a person to look within himself in order to verify himself and understand himself. Without turning inward, a person cannot truly understand himself. If he cannot understand himself, how is he meant to bring him true self to human relationships? Furthermore, he can feel confused and disappointed in many things throughout his life. He is a stranger to himself.

Understand this: very little of the brain is created with the assistance of the education system. The unconscious mind, that which is unrevealed to a person as he lives his reality, is a vast land of the unknown. It holds a person's dreams; it holds reminiscence of all of a person's experiences. It provides so many of the biases and reasons a person does everything he does. With meditation, a person can finally tap into this bizarre realm and begin to understand himself in the pulsing strangeness of his interior consciousness.

An untrained, un-meditative mind is restless and gets in the way of meditation habits. Therefore, in order to experience the essential nature of himself, a person must work beyond the brain's unruly nature. Without working beyond the restless mind, a person's meditative state is only a string of daydreams and fantastical hallucinations. He cannot experience the mind stillness required to achieve meditation.

Creating Mind Stillness

Reveal mind stillness in yourself by attending to your brain. Sit with your back straight, your neck holding your head high. You should be in a quiet, clean place, completely alone. Take a few deep breaths and focus your mind on attending to your body. Allow each of your muscles to relax from your head to your toes. Take your time. Feel your tension fall away from each muscle. You are beginning to let go of your concrete self.

Next, bring your awareness to your breathing techniques—just as you did with your mindfulness techniques. Breathe in and out while feeling which parts of your brain move. Feel your diaphragm moving in and out. Try to accept each breath as it comes and not to ask yourself if you're breathing "correctly." Simply be.

Listen to your brain and what it is telling you. Is it racing? Is it asking you when you can be done meditating, when you can finally go downstairs and watch television? Is it tossing and turning? Your brain is constantly doing this as you maneuver through your daily life. However, if you listen to your brain and its "demands" in your meditative state, you will feel no sense of urgency. You will refute action to these demands and give your whirring brain no power.

Finally, you will feel the interior freedom from your whirring brain. You will accept what your churning brain has to say, and you will feel it pass before you. You will give it no meaning. As you vacation from these whirring reminders and thoughts, you can push beyond to an inner sense of peace and relief. You can finally relieve yourself from the constant journey of the rest of your life.

As you rest in this inner unconscious mind, you can train your mind to accept the exterior world and live better while in it. Think about this: you are able to ignore the whirring mind that is attempting you to come away from your current meditative goals. And yet, usually, you listen to each one of those thoughts. Much in the same way, you consistently listen to people in your exterior settings. When they put you down, you listen and you alter your feelings about your day. You are in tune, generally, with the immediate stressors of whatever's around you.

However, if you hold within you these meditative abilities to ignore that which brings you stress and tumult, you can analyze your feelings and preciously why you are feeling them. You can feel anger, for example, and understand how you can dismiss this anger.

Therefore, through the process of meditation, you can become far more balanced in your exterior life. You can expose—to yourself, most importantly—your inner immaturities and your improper habits. You can become fully aware of yourself and the ways in which you can change your life for the better.

Your meditation benefits will reveal themselves slowly and surely. Make sure to take time for meditation every day at whichever time you feel most susceptible to self-honesty. Keep your mind focused on each and every experience of your life, and understand the ways in which you're reacting to these experiences. Feel yourself relax in your daily life, and find yourself experiencing the simple joys of being completely present.

Chapter 4. Yoga: Techniques and Historical Context

The term "yoga" brings mental, physical, and spiritual practices together to yield transcendence on both mental and physical levels. Several separate spiritual sects have developed and utilized yoga for their own benefits; it stems from Hinduism, Jainism, and Buddhism. The actual word is quite literal; it springs from "yoking together" oxen or horses. However, it is now applied to bringing together the body and the mind: a sort of yoking, if you will.

History of Yoga

Learn the ways in which yoga has brought aide to the human condition for countless centuries. It is, perhaps, as old as spirituality itself.

The first known record of yoga is found in several stone seals that reveal classic yoga poses. These stones were formulated as early as 3,000 B.C. However, anthropologists peg the first years of yoga to the beginnings of the Stone Age Shamanism. Remember the shamans of the previous chapters; they were meant to be closer to the "source" of spirituality, and thus could bring a sort of "enlightenment" to the greater population. Through these poses, the shaman could perhaps bring healing and greater senses of religion to his people. He could bring the community together.

After these ancient years, however, yoga split into four distinct periods: the Vedic Period, the Pre-Classical Period, the Classical Period, and the Post-Classical Period.

The Vedic Period

The basis of modern-day Hinduism teachings is found in a scripture called the Vedas. The Vedas brings a collection of ancient hymns that declare glory to a higher power. Also included in this book are the oldest written Yoga instructions. The book gives instructions for various ceremonies and rituals to provide perfect Yoga environments.

The Vedic Period brought great Yogis teachers who held a deep connection between their minds and bodies. Rishis, one sort of teacher, held the ability to view ultimate reality. In Buddhism, this "ultimate reality" is referred to as Nirvana.

During the Vedic Period, Yogis wrote for the first time about the spiritual wonders of living in complete seclusion in forests, as well. The benefits of seclusion have been linked to spiritualism since this very ancient time.

Pre-Classical Yoga

Pre-Classical Yoga churned from the written text, the Upanishads. The Upanishads is two hundred scriptures that bring the inner "vision" of ultimate reality. The description includes three ideas: the ultimate reality, the transcendental individual, and the general relationship between the ultimate reality and the transcendental individual.

Also during this time, Siddharta Gautauma began teaching yoga. He was the first Buddhist to do so.

The Classical Period

The Classical Period of Yoga churned from the creation of the Yoga Sutra, written in the second century by a man named Patanjali. The Yoga Sutra outlines the "Eightfold Path of Yoga" or the "Eight Limbs of Classical Yoga."

1. Yama: social restraints and ingrained ethics.
2. Niyama: interior observation of tolerance, purity, and study.
3. Asanas: physical, bodily exercises.
4. Pranayama: breath control.
5. Pratyahara: withdrawal from the mind in order to find Meditation.
6. Dharana: finding concentration.
7. Dhyana: Meditation.
8. Samadhi: ecstasy.

Patanjali, the scribe of the Yoga Sutra, actually differed greatly from his past yogis. Instead of writing about the relationship of the body and the mind, he saw them as two separate entities. He believed that everyone was made of a spirit and a bunch of matter. He believed the two should remain separate entities so that the spirit could be clean.

During this time, meditation was practiced almost exclusively, and the asanas—or physical practices—were dismissed. After several centuries, the "body as a temple" idea came back into favor, and the exercises took their form.

Post-Classical Yoga

Yoga finds its way into the western hemisphere and brings a complete difference from its first three periods. Instead of liberating a person from his reality, Yoga chooses instead to allow a person to accept his reality. He is able, through Yoga practices, to accept both himself and himself in relation to his greater environment.

Yoga arrived to the western hemisphere in the 19th century. It was initially studied as a separate entity: as a bizarre mechanism from a different culture. However, the surge of vegetarianism in the 1930's produced an interest in the ancient craft. Yoga grew exponentially.

One of the modern teachers of the 1960's was named Swami Sivananda. He eventually modified the Five Principles of Yoga:

1. Savasana: proper and ultimate relaxation.
2. Asanas: proper and ultimate exercise.
3. Pranayama: proper and fulfilled breathing.
4. Nutritious Diet.
5. Dhyana: Proper and positive thinking.

YOGA POSES AND BENEFITS

Asanas is the utilization of yoga exercises in order to assimilate the connection between your body and your mind. Look to the following poses to target specific parts of your body and bring a sense of oneness, a sense of connection to your interior unconsciousness. Remember that your body is one of the things inhibiting you from your interior understanding of yourself, as well. When you eliminate interior pains by stretching your body, you can bring a sense of calm to your exterior and work to study your mind.

DANDASANA OR STAFF POSE

This yoga pose strengthens your posture. Better posture has been shown to lead to a greater sense of positivity.

Sit on the floor with your back completely straight. Your legs should be stretched out in front of you, side-by-side with your toes up toward the sky. Place your arms flat to your sides. This may seem incredibly simple. However, you'll begin to feel the stretch and the power behind the pose.

Marjaryasana or *Cat pose*

This yoga pose alleviates stress and reduces your fight or flight hormone, cortisol.

Place your hands out on the ground with your arms straight up in the air like you're about to do a push up. Bring your knees comfortably to the ground, directly below your knees, and arch your back like a cat as you exhale. As you inhale, bring your spine back to a tabletop formation. You should feel a massage to your belly organs and your spine. Your eyes should look toward the floor.

Uttanasana or *Standing Forward Bend*

This yoga pose alleviates stress and actively stretches your hamstrings.

As you stand, drape yourself over at the hips and grasp your legs as low as you can. Lengthen your torso as you descend slowly. Try to place your hands on the floor and stand in a folded-over position. Your hamstrings will begin to loosen, and your mind will feel calm. As you inhale, lengthen your torso. As you exhale, push yourself just a bit more into the bend.

Salamba Sirsasana or Head Stand with Support

The supported headstand brings much-needed blood and oxygen to your brain and allows you to think well and transcend your exterior environment. It further assists in strengthening your arms and legs, while improving your digestion. It beats back against stress and depression, and provides a firm, toned abdomen.

Fold out a blanket or mat and kneel on the floor. After you lace your fingers together, set your forearms on the mat with your elbows situated about a shoulder's width apart. Place your head's crown directly on the floor in the center of those elbows. Place the back of your head against your clasped hands.

Next, bring your knees off the floor and walk your feet closer and closer to your head. Ultimately lift your feet from the ground with the strength from your thighs. Make sure to remove both of your feet from the floor at the same time, exhaling soundly. Align your body so that it is straight. Make sure, for example, that your tailbone is firm against your pelvis.

Remember to keep your weight even across your shoulder blades. During your first stint, maintain this pose for just ten seconds. As you increase your abilities, add five seconds.

Chapter 5. Finding Inner Peace

Inner peace is that which all the great religions and spiritual doctrines are searching for. Inner peace is the state of complete mental and spiritual peace. The person with inner peace has an understanding of himself that allows him to work through stressors, to acknowledge his feelings and piece through them. This "peace" is considered a general homeostasis; therefore, peace is the antithesis of stress and anxiety. It folds into its relation with happiness, bliss, and contentment.

Many communities and cultures reach toward this inner peace through forms of meditation, prayer, and various exercises like T'ai Chi Ch'uan or yoga. Both Hinduism and Buddhism search for this inner peace through their various practices; the religious doctrines understand that knowing one's self is the greatest inner peace in the world.

Self-Actualization

A term often linked with inner piece is "self-actualization." Self-actualization stems from various psychological theories, and was originally coined by Kurt Goldstein so many, many centuries after the first yoga masters took their first pretzel formations. The theories state, generally, that a person's life is only fulfilled through self-actualization. Self-actualization involves understanding one's abilities and life purpose and utilizing those abilities to gain one's potentiality.

By reaching this high realm of potentially, a person is said to utilize all creative and spiritual tendencies. Therefore, if a person has a potential to be an artist, that person absolutely must utilize his artistic talents to reach his self-actualization. He must actualize himself using his great abilities.

Scholars understand that people who follow paths that force them to utilize different skills—skill that do not work through these special talents that they've been gifted with—are generally unhappy and find a lack of meaning in their lives. Their happiness levels are much lower than those who know themselves, know their talents, and reach toward their goals with joie de vivre.

However, as outlined in other chapters, a person must understand himself on a very interior level and block out other stressors and distractions in order to fuel himself with the understanding of what he must do in order to self-actualize. He can do this through meditation, through mindfulness, and through yoga techniques. He must calm his mind, calm his body, and find the inner solace of simply "being." Only then can he view the world as a place of separate, intricate events: not a mad, rushing world in which he has no choice of where he goes.

When the meditative man steps back, he can achieve a better mental state with regards to the surrounding world. He can think about a certain scenario and consider if this scenario fits into his inner solace's plan for greater strength and spirituality. For example, if he finds that a job simply does not fulfill his purpose, he can look inside himself and find that he would be unhappy with that job position. A person without inner solace and strength might find himself struggling with decisions, uncertain of where to turn. He might make a rash decision.

Achieving self-actualization is a great step toward inner peace, just as inner peace allows a person to maintain better self-actualization. It's a constantly rotating spectrum, allowing a person to live a rejuvenated, meaningful life.

Chapter 6.
Achieving Enlightenment

Enlightenment is the ultimate goal of the Buddhist faith. The English language has arched the term "enlightenment" across several different Buddhist terminologies. However, enlightenment refers most specifically to several different spiritual terms Bodhi, nirvana, prajna, knesho, and satori. Enlightenment is the end of the Buddhist path and is often described as the full reach toward knowledge of both one's self and the greater world.

Bodhi, the Buddhist term, literally means "to have woken up to an understanding." Prajna refers to the actual nature of the knowledge the Buddha found upon waking up to understanding. Most notably, this knowledge brings about the three marks of existence. As mentioned before, these three marks are: impermanence, or the feeling of one's body's impermanence; the unsatisfactory nature of all surrounding, worldly elements; and an achievement of non-self or a reach toward something beyond one's whirring brain. Through complete understanding, or "Bodhi" of these three terms, one is said to have achieved the end of one's suffering.

Siddharth, the great Buddha known to have achieved "enlightenment," chose to describe the three marks of existence this way:

Anicca, or impermanence: All things are constantly changing or in flux. Therefore, nothing has ever ceased to exist; it simply has changed. Appearances change. A leaf falls to the ground from a tree, but its cells go on to form new plants and new trees. Nothing is ever really gone.

Dukkha or dissatisfaction: Nothing physical or material can bring the utmost satisfaction that one searches for.

Anatta, or non-self: This element of Buddhism refers to the body as something without self. If refers to all the elements of the world as temporal things, things that hold no "soul-like" brevity. It notes that all mental, brain processes are completely impermanent. It frees one from the feeling of one's self, allowing one to look at the greater, surrounding picture.

Buddhism and Nirvana

Ultimately, of course, once these three marks are achieved, one is meant to achieve "nirvana," another word grouped in the concept of enlightenment. Nirvana is the ideal state in which the spirit is ultimately free from the constant cycles of life and death, over and over. According to Buddhist tradition, Gautama Buddha, the Buddha, reached Nirvana as he sat beneath a Bodhi tree. He was completely free from his surrounding world; he was completely free from human suffering, anger, and lust.

Achieve Enlightenment Today

When you achieve enlightenment, you are said to have transcended all religious doctrines. You have found a reason beyond life or death. You can dissolve the boundaries between every stereotype, and you can truly look at yourself as a non-entity, as a being part of the greater world. You can find freedom from your whirring mind and achieve ultimate relaxation. Your current limited understanding about the greater world and universe is holding you back from ultimate peace. Find complete awareness of everything, and be in the very present moment at all times. Meld together with a formation of knowledge, intelligence, and deep love, and feel like a truly changed person.

The path to enlightenment must involve intention. That is, it doesn't just "happen" without your intense effort. Beyond this intention, however, there are several worldwide disciplines designed to charge you toward an enlightened path.

1. *MEDITATION.*

    Meditation is outlined more in depth in Chapter 3. Disciplined meditation brings a calming of your mind; it allows you to bring conscious attention to yourself as you eliminate your focus from everything else. As you cut down on your external distractions, you can begin to focus on eliminating your internal distractions, as well.

    Different Enlightenment Meditative Paths:

    A. Mindfulness and Meditation: This stems from the Buddhist tradition and is the most prevalent version outlined in this book. In Buddhism, this is called "Vipassana," and refers to the focus of being precisely in the moment, in the present, allowing your mind to run and run without your judgment. As you observe your thoughts, you begin to detach yourself from those thoughts. Therefore, your brain doesn't create a "string" of related thoughts; it no longer perpetuates the madness. Instead, the brain becomes quiet.

B. Sitting and Meditation: This stems from the Zen tradition and is called Zazen. Zen is a practical Buddhism, designed to bring you toward enlightenment; it is further outlined later in this chapter. Most notably, however, Zen tradition asks a sort of "riddle" of the mind that is supposed to cause a slight hiccup. This hiccup is meant to transmit confusion; it is meant to stop the brain's whirring altogether. An example of this is: "If a tree falls in the forest, will anyone hear it?" There's no possible way to answer this question.

C. Walking Meditation: This type of meditation is a form of action-oriented meditation. The actual experience of walking is meant to be your focus. You think only of the walk, of your body's movements. This is a generally "easier" form of meditation in that you are able to parse out the feelings of your body much better as you glide around; at least, you can feel your body so much better than when you sit. Beyond being easier, however, walking meditation can be incredibly intense as you experience your muscles, your bones, your everything in a new light.

D. Kundalini: This type of meditation is outlined in more detail in the yoga chapter. Kundalini means "coiled." When you coil yourself, practice yoga, you can bring about the life energy at the base of your spine. This "life energy" is often felt as heat; as the coiled energy of your spine rises along your energy centers, or "chakras," you can ultimately feel that life energy in your brain. Energy in your brain produces enlightened feelings.

2. *PRAYER.*

Today's investment in prayer brings about the wrong idea. Prayer today is a plea, a cry for assistance, a conversation attempted with a higher power, or some sort of recitation of a verse. This is absolutely wrong and achieves no greater, interior spirituality. Rather, prayer is meant to be a silent contemplation and a listen for a feeling of a higher power.

Proper prayer needs a silent mind, a mind that holds peace and understands its meditative states. As the mind waits for god's voice, the mind feels blissful grace. This feeling of grace is often described as enlightenment, or a feeling of intense knowledge and truth.

Catholic tradition actually brings attention to the silent mind. It utilizes prayer beads and thus allows you to focus on a single prayer, on just a few words, to bring calmness to your mind. Focusing on a single thing is just a few steps away from focusing on nothing at all. With focus nothing at all, you can achieve enlightenment.

This could be a reason that Jesus, the Christian god, reduced his prayer to a single prayer: the Lord's Prayer. It was meant to allow his disciples to focus on simply one thing and perhaps feel that unity with god by nearly eliminating all conscious thought.

3. *CHANTING.*

As mentioned previously, chanting is one of the oldest spiritual tricks on the road to feeling at one with a higher power, on the journey to enlightenment. Chants come in all shapes, all melodies; however, they generally form with a great deal of repetition.

Chanting is utilized from Hawaii, to Africa, to Native American cultures, to the Qur'an, to the chanting of prayers in the Roman Catholic Church. These chanting practices vary from Buddhist throat singing to Hindu mantras. The Hare Kirshna movement, for example, brings about a focus on chanting Snaskrit Names of God.

Chanting further brings about the idea that you are focusing on only one thing; one thing is just a short step from nothing.

4. *MARTIAL ARTS.*

   Martial arts allow enlightenment with strenuous physical activity of repetitive body motions. Each motion requires intense mental discipline. The inner-mind focused martial arts include Budo, Tai Chi, and Qigong. As your body moves, your mind becomes quiet and focused only on your body. You can reduce your conscious thought and come further to the idea of enlightenment.

5. *FASTING.*

   Fasting has been a long-touted concept that is meant to improve your chances of reaching enlightenment. For example, Jesus fasted for a full forty days according to the Bible, while Siddartha Guatama, the first Buddha, also fasted. Ramadan, the Islamic holy period, requires continued fasting while the sun is up, while Judaism requires fasting during Yom Kippur.

   Because food is absolutely necessary to keep your body functioning, you must, in essence, indulge in it every single day. Therefore, it becomes a sort of god to you: it is your continued source of energy. As you work against this utilization of food, your mind must work to find a different sort of enlightenment. Your mind will find the spiritual "food" of its god.

6. *Sweat Lodges.*

   Native Americans practiced the sweat lodge traditions for several centuries in order to communicate with spirits and achieve internal enlightenment. While in a sweat lodge, the body falls into distress due to its loss of water and the high temperatures. The brain becomes distressed, as well, and thought becomes less patterned. With fewer streams of consciousness, the brain can become far more focused and achieve enlightenment.

7. *Quaking and Shaking.*

   The man who founded the Quaker Religion, George Fox, was an enlightened man. He stated that god dwelt in a person's heart, and that the body was the ultimate temple. To achieve enlightenment through the Quaker faith, you are meant to dance and move and "quake" until you reach complete physical exhaustion. Through exhaustion, the brain cannot "think" as well. Shakers, another religious sect, also find themselves closer to god as they shake on their prayerful quests.

8. *Pilgrimage.*

   Several spiritual religions call for pilgrimages in order to follow the path of enlightenment. Through the pilgrimage, you are meant to release your sense of ego, or your sense of yourself. As you release your sense of self, you can find all layers of yourself—you can uncover your true life's meaning.

While on a pilgrimage, you are escaping your familiar backdrop or the very things that remind you, continually, of the illusion of who you think you are. A step outside of these boundaries, therefore, is necessary to see yourself clearly.

Examples of required religious pilgrimages are the visit the Mecca in the Islamic tradition and the travel to Jerusalem in the Jewish tradition. Furthermore, Buddhists climb mountains in order to sit in sacred temples.

During a pilgrimage, you do not release your consciousness. However, an achievement of reducing your sense of self lies on the path to enlightenment and is eternally important.

THE ZEN MIND

Zen is a school of Buddhism developed in sixth century China. Unlike several other religious doctrines, Zen brings the focus away from intellectual teachings. According to Zen tradition, these doctrines actually bring about notions of one's appearance and thus work against transcendental wisdom. Much like the rest of Buddhism, Zen allows one to turn one's eye inward and to analyze one's self. The Zen Mind is also the Enlightened mind.

OBSERVE THE MIND AND OBSERVE THE BREATH

During Zen meditation, a person sits in lotus and analyzes his breathing techniques. He feels his breath go in and out of his body, and also places his energy in the arena beneath his naval. Furthermore, after he analyzes the mind, he works to become aware of his conscious thoughts. Through analysis of his thoughts, he can begin to refute them as things that do not control him.

THE KOAN PRACTICE

The Koan practice is often utilized in the Zen tradition. Essentially, Koan practices bring a question or a riddle from the Zen master to the Zen student in order to analyze if the student is learning properly. These riddles or questions look to probe the mind of these students and also present a sort of puzzle to further deepen the mind and reach toward a better sense of enlightenment.

Examples of traditional koans include:

Does a dog have a Buddhist nature or not? The student is meant to say, absolutely, no.

What is the sound of one hand clapping? To answer this question, the student must understand that the activity of koan is the very search of the answer to koan. Therefore, koan is what is being sought and it is further the act of seeking. Therefore, one hand clapping is actually two hands clapping each other because two hands have become one in this koan scenario.

Chapter 7. Spiritual Healing

Spiritual healing is an internal healing process, one that strides alongside contemporary medicines in order to bring overall health. It is thought that one can achieve power toward wiping out one's diseases and disabilities through the concepts of prayer and spirituality. Oftentimes, these spiritual healing practices are ritualistic in nature. It's important to note, of course, that a doctor is necessary for all physical assistance; however, spiritual healing can complement this physical assistance and bring life affirming qualities and strength.

Spiritual healing is orchestrated through every religious doctrine and through all secular peoples. It chooses to boost non-physical elements of the body such as the emotions, the mind, and the general "life force."

Engage in Spiritual Healing

In order to bring yourself to spiritual healing, you must be completely open to it. You must have a certain degree of trust in the person attempting to administer spiritual healing to you. Your positive attitude with regards to your interior being actually brings greater strength to the spiritual healing process than any other element.

When you begin the Spiritual Healing process, the healer will ask you to become completely comfortable. You will, for example, remove your coat, your spectacles. You'll turn off your hearing aid and sit on a comfortable couch or chair. Afterwards, the healer will oftentimes place his hands on you or very near to you.

With his hands close to you or touching you, the healer will ask you to begin to quiet and relax your mind. He will ask you to close your eyes. As you do this, you must remember not to think about what is happening to you. You must remove yourself from the settings, just as you've read in the other sections. You must allow your mind to recede into the background. It is thought, then, that the healer transmits certain positive energies into you to promote your internal healing.

Therapeutic Touch

Therapeutic touch is a type of spiritual healing, or energy healing, utilized today. Nurse practitioners claim that therapeutic touch reduces patient pain and anxiety. Furthermore, they proclaim that it promotes patient healing. They engage in therapeutic touch by placing their hands on a patient and "manipulating" that patient's energy. This therapeutic touch holds its roots in ancient healing practices like the laying on of hands. Because it is a type of spiritual healing, it holds no root in religion.

Reiki

Reiki is a recent Buddhist development that utilizes several traditions like palm healing or hands-on healing to bring complementary, spiritual healing. These practitioners believe they're transferring energy to bring equilibrium to their patients. They further believe that this energy is generally intelligent and can therefore fuel from their fingers to the precise, designated spots in the body that require healing. Reiki understands that there are seven "chakras" or positions of greater energy in the body. It therefore centers itself on these chakras to push the most energy throughout the body.

Because the mind and body are so linked in many secular and religious spiritual realms, the concept of both Reiki and Therapeutic Touch in the overall umbrella of spiritual healing is not a great stretch. If the mind becomes balanced through the exchange of energies, the mind can transmit this power of balance to the rest of the body. The mind has complete and utter control over the body if the mind practices and utilizes all of its sectors. Control of the mind, mindfulness, or even another person's therapeutic mindfulness, can bring about internal healing.

Spirituality: A Conclusion

Spirituality is the ultimate search for meaning in the utter confusion that is daily life. Ancient traditions and current traditions hold so many similarities, leaving the understanding that the search for meaning is never truly finished. However, the simple journey, the ultimate reach toward this betterment of one's life reveals so much about one's interior self. One can understand one's purpose; one can calm one's self and reduce anxiety. One can live more fruitfully. With spirituality in one's interior self, one can truly live with purpose.

About The Author

My mission with this is to be able to help inspire and change the world, one reader at a time.

I want to provide the most amazing life tools that anyone can apply into their lives. It doesn't matter whether you have hit rock bottom in your life or your life is amazing and you want to keep taking it to another level.

If you are like me, then you are probably looking to become the best version of yourself. You are likely not to settle for an okay life. You want to live an extraordinary life. Not only to be filled within but also to contribute to society.

OTHER BOOKS BY JUSTIN ALBERT

Personal Growth for Teens: Discover Yourself and Become Who You Want

Personal Growth and Inspiration: Achieve Greatness in Everything You Do

FREE PREVIEW OF

MOTIVATION:

GETTING MOTIVATED, FEELING MOTIVATED, STAYING MOTIVATED

JUSTIN ALBERT

Copyright © 2014 by Justin Albert

Why You Should Read This Book

Motivation provides ultimate life fulfillment. It is the driving force behind every profession, every physical action. It fuels the creation of towering skyscrapers, five-star restaurant, and stellar paintings—

And yet: why is motivation so difficult to attain and maintain? Another thing: why is it so difficult to get out of bed? When did life get so out of hand?

This book analyzes these questions on both a scientific and emotional level. It lends the proper tools to build motivation in the wake of utter difficulty.

Motivation is pumping in every blood vessel, through every neuron. Human ancestors struggling to survive in the wild were fueled with this instinct: this motivation to persevere. Present people still pulse with this very intrinsic motivation. However, present-day people—because their needs are generally met, their food is generally supplied—must work for their motivation. They must keep eyes open; they must create their own understanding of their goals. Their goal is no longer: survive. Their goal is to prosper.

Procrastination. Stress. The dog needs walking, the cat needs fed. The work piles up, and motivation for desires and interests is simply out of reach. This Motivation E-book teaches the art of catching desires and interests once again and persevering. It outlines the ways one can work through the blocks in your path and attain that promotion, achieve that great legacy. One must do this: reach for real, vibrant goals in order to attain real destiny—to know self-actualization. Only with self-actualization can one feel a renewed sense of prosperity, a full sense of self.

Chapter 1. Motivation: The Only Road to Greatness

Humankind's all-inclusive goal is, effectively, one thing: to survive. The survival concept lurks behind all things in a person's life: behind every kitchen product, behind every home improvement store. And yet, naturally, this survival has changed over the years. It has diminished from something broad, something that must meet required caloric values and required habitat-levels into something much more refined.

What is, then, man's essential, present-day goal? To simply live. And to live well. To live better than man has before. And this goal requires innovation; it requires a push against the limits surrounding each person's life. Without breadth of motivation, people would not leave their beds; they wouldn't work to find a better life. Without motivation, people would have nothing.

Motivation is the call to action. It is the thing that pushes one from one's bed to greet the world and squeeze every ounce of energy from it. It is the thing that forces one to take one's proper stance in the world.

Do you feel, today, that you have the depth of motivation to reach your goals, to push yourself to the top of your career and become a prime person—a person with both physical and mental strength? Do you have the will to survive and the motivation to make the most of that survival?

Understand motivation and the current factors blocking you

from your complete embrace of your goals. Understand the ways in which you can become the best version of yourself.

WHAT IS MOTIVATION?

Understanding the precise utilization of motivation is essential in order to prescribe everyday life goals; prescribing life goals via motivation allows for forward-motion.

DEFINITION OF MOTIVATION

Motivation, essentially, is that which initiates and maintains goal-driven mannerisms. It is an unseen force. Biological, cognitive, and social effects alter motivation; these forces mold it, form it into something that either allows growth or stagnation.

Biological effects on motivation involve the various mechanisms required at a very physical level. As aforementioned, one has kitchen appliances that rev and whir in order to maintain a very base biological motive: to boost one's caloric intake for further survival. One reaches for a glass of Coca Cola, essentially, out of motivation to quench one's thirst. These motives are incredibly basic and biological; the animals and plants of the earth have similar biological motivations, as well. A human simply has refined his reach to maintain these motivations.

Cognitive effects on motivation are incredibly complicated. Hormonal imbalances, the things one eats and the things by which one is surrounded can affect the brain, thus altering one's motivational output. Depression, stress, and low self-esteems accumulate at this cognitive level and impair judgment, thus altering continued rev for motivation.

Social effects on motivation generally involve one's environment and cultural influence. What is expected of one in one's culture generally contributes to one's sense of motivation; for example, history finds women generally staying home with children. Their motivation could not grow due to social influences. Furthermore, one's parents and one's friends alter social motivation. If one lives in a stagnant environment—an environment featuring people without conscious effort, without conscious forward-motion, one might simply assimilate into this way of life. However, if one's parents expect certain successes, social motivation might be the factor contributing to one's college graduation, for example.

THREE COMPONENTS OF MOTIVATION

1) Activation
2) Persistence
3) Intensity

Activation is the primary component: the decision to begin. A person must make this conscious decision; it is the root of all motivation. It is the very thing that allows mature motivation to grow. For example, actively enrolling in an exercise class activates the motivation to become healthy and lose weight, thus improving one's life.

Persistence is the continuation of this activation. It involves one's push through obstacles after the initial activation. It involves intense, psychological strength. For example, after one enrolls in the exercise class with the obvious intention of becoming healthy and thin, persistence must step in to truly fuel motivation. After the exercise class begins, one must invest endless hours, limitless concentration, and physicality to the point of exhaustion. It is increasingly difficult to maintain the intensity. However, if one is fueled with the proper motivation, working through the exercise class until completion garners significant strength and benefits.

Finally, intensity measures one's level of vigor after initially activating and persisting. If one persists through the various exercise classes, for example, without a significant level of concentration and exertion, one is not truly motivated. One can persist, certainly. But one will not reach the final goal of true health and strength without full-throttle intensity. Find another example in university-level classes. One can activate one's enrollment; one can attend every class; but if one does not fuel every day with study and push one's self outside of class, one will probably not achieve maximum success.

Extrinsic Motivation versus Intrinsic Motivation

Motivation is found both extrinsically and intrinsically.

Extrinsic motivation exists outside the individual. Usually, it involves the motivation to pursue exterior rewards or trophies—things resulting from successes involving other people. Therefore, extrinsic motivation involves motivation from peers; it involves impressing others via one's success. One's competitive desire can drive this extrinsic motivation completely.

Intrinsic motivation, on the other hand, exists internally. The internal gratification of completing a very personal project, for example, fuels this intrinsic motivation. Perhaps one wants to finish cleaning and decorating one's bedroom simply to feel the fresh, open understanding that one's habitat is for one's self; one's habitat reflects one's life, after all. However, if one simply wants to decorate one's room in order to impress another person, this could deem extrinsic motivation. Essentially, if one is the sole operator of one's motivation without exterior benefit, one is fueled with intrinsic motivation.

A Life Without Motivation: What Happens?

What happens without that pulsing drive of motivation? Where does this lack of motivation lead? Remember that motivation is the building block for all survival, all strength in existence. Furthermore, it is the real push behind desire and interest. It is the very thing that fuels the beautiful paintings in museums, the towering skyscrapers, and the countless football games. It is human's driving force toward the meaning of life.

Feelings of Failure and Inadequacy

Without motivation, one cannot move forward with one's life. One must remain stagnant. Essentially, one's hometown becomes one's only town. One's first job becomes one's only job. Lack of motivation leads nowhere.

But this lack of push does not lead to a lack of feeling. Emotion is always at play. In fact, emotion is generally the pulse behind lack of motivation. These emotions come in forms like fear of failure, fear of the unknown, incredible stresses, and low self-esteem. If one cannot work through these emotions, one cannot build a solid motivational ground. And without this ground and garnered goals, failure and inadequacy sweep into the emotional mix. One can feel a loss: like the past few years of one's life went toward nothing. One can feel a desire to do it all over again—with that drive of motivation at their backs. Unfortunately, lost years don't come back around. And inadequacy and feelings of failure linger.

Fortunately, these feelings of inadequacy can be the very reason to push toward motivation and reach toward something else. Proper use of feelings is always important. Work toward the promotion you haven't even dreamed about; wonder why you never thought to go to the gym. Understand that there's a whole world out there waiting for you. Claim it.

Chapter 2. Theories of Motivation

Psychologists' motivation analysis involves several theories. They analyze the precise reasons why one is fueled with motivation—and why one may have difficulty jumping on the motivation train.

Drive Theory

Behaviorist Clark Hull created the drive reduction theory of motivation in the 1940s and 1950s. He was one of the first scientists to attempt to understand the broad depth of human motivation.

Homeostasis: Balance and Equilibrium

Hull's theories attend to the facts of homeostasis. Homeostasis is the fact that one's body constantly works to achieve balance, equilibrium. For example, one's body finds a consistent, approximate temperature of 98.6 degrees Fahrenheit. When one dips below or above this number, one's body hustles to achieve balance once more.

Essentially, the "drive" of drive theory refers to the tension aroused by the imbalance or lack of homeostasis in one's body. In the temperature case, therefore, one's interior drive is the fact that one's temperature is out of whack. Further drives are hunger and thirst. These drives, or stimuli, force one's body into action to achieve balance in the form of a meal or a glass of water.

Therefore, Hull's drive theory acts on a sort of stimulus-response mechanism. His theory is rooted in biology and therefore takes no notice of interior, life goals. However, he does provide a decent understanding of the root of motivation.

INSTINCT THEORY

Psychologist William McDougall studied the instinct theory in relation to human motivation. His essential findings rooted the instinct theory as a way through life—a way that assured continuation of life via natural selection. Of course, the behaviors he studied were not limited to biological needs. He studied human instinct; and human instinct garners several shades of gray.

WHAT IS AN INSTINCT?

An instinct involves a tendency to behave in a specific manner without engaging in thought. The acts are spontaneous, occurring in a sort of matter of course after a particular occurrence.

Human instincts cover a broad range of occurrences rooted in both physiological and psychological needs. Physiological motivations, of course, meet hunger, thirst, and habitation needs. Psychological motivations, however, clasp something a bit more human; things like: humor, curiosity, cleanliness, fear, anger, shame, and love.

MASLOW'S HIERARCHY OF NEEDS

Abraham Maslow's humanistic theory of motivation analyzes all the basic human elements—from the simplistic biological needs to the self-actualization needs.

He breaks these needs into five stages with the idea that one's motivations can only escalate when one's needs are met at the immediate stages.

Stage 1: Physiological Needs

As aforementioned, physiological needs consist of the basic, survival needs like water, food, and sleep. One must meet these physiological needs prior to building the motivation to move to the next step.

Stage 2: Safety Needs

These safety needs involve providing one's self with proper health, income, and an actual "home."

Stage 3: Love/Belonging Needs

After one meets physiological needs and one has a place to live, a place in which to feel whole, one can begin to understand the benefits of social surroundings. These benefits can fall from familial ties, friendship, work groups—anything that forms a sort of relationship in which one can beat back against loneliness and find a place in society.

Stage 4: Self-Esteem Needs

One jumps to the self esteem needs stage in the convenient stage after one feels a sense of belonging. Learning that one "fits" in a society is a great link in the chain. Self-esteem needs allow one the motivation to achieve in one's school or work and to build one's reputation. It allows one to take responsibility of other things or other people. This is essential in the hierarchy of needs: that one does not "need" anything anymore—one is motivated, instead, to help other people meet their needs. One is further motivated to meet one's wants.

Stage 5: Self-Actualization Needs

Self-actualization involves something a bit deeper than the self-esteem stage. The self-esteem stage requires one to achieve in society, to take charge of one's self and one's life. However, the self-actualization stage motivates one to find personal growth, it motivates one to feel fulfilled by one's career, one's relationships. It might not be enough, for example, for one to simply achieve at one's job. This stage might require one to feel as if one's commitment to one's job is also making the world a better place, for example. One might do some soul-searching in this stage to truly understand one's place in the world. One cannot commit to this true soul-searching, of course, without meeting the initial four stages of the hierarchy of needs. However, to truly find one's self and truly meet one's goals, one must exist at this top stage—with all other needs completed.

Keep reading...

MOTIVATION:

GETTING MOTIVATED, FEELING MOTIVATED, STAYING MOTIVATED

ONE LAST THING...

If you enjoyed this book or found it useful I'd be very grateful if you'd post a short review on Amazon. Your support really does make a difference and I read all the reviews personally so I can get your feedback and make this book even better.

Thanks again for your support!

14574376R00044

Printed in Poland
by Amazon Fulfillment
Poland Sp. z o.o., Wrocław